A PREPARATION, PRACTICE AND PAUSE GUIDEBOOK

Copyright (c) 2022, Jessyca Vandercoy, LCSW and Alicia Webber, LICSW.
LIBRARY OF CONGRESS CATALOGING-IN-PUBLICATION DATA
Vandercoy, Jessyca; Webber, Alicia
Pause.: A preparation, practice and pause guidebook
ISBN: 979-8-218-11696-5

Content adapted from:
LIBRARY OF CONGRESS CATALOGING-IN-PUBLICATION DATA
Vandercoy, Jessyca; Webber, Alicia; Konwinski, Amie
Unplug and Be Present: An activity journey into taking a social media pause.

PAUSE.

A PREPARATION, PRACTICE AND PAUSE GUIDEBOOK

This activity journey was built for humans;
journalers and artists,
doodlers and dreamers,
logical and emotional,
teens and adults.

It was built for YOU!

This activity journey belongs to:

OUR STORY

The creators of this activity book have embarked on the same journey you are about to. We have paused, reduced, and changed our relationship with our devices and social media. We've experienced the challenges, gifts, and emotions that come with realigning our thoughts and behaviors to reduce the power social media has in our lives. The benefits were great and we started supporting others in this change.

The creators and illustrators come with some pretty cool personal and professional experiences. We all identify as women and hold many other identities including athlete, mentor, entrepreneur, business owner, mother, clinician, social worker, military veteran, tech guru, student, educator, and yoga instructor. We took what we learned from our experiences, along with our professional expertise, and created this preparation, practice and pause guidebook for you.

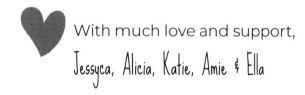

With much love and support,
Jessyca, Alicia, Katie, Amie & Ella

Whole Collective
Co-Creators: Jessyca Vandercoy, LCSW & Alicia Webber, LICSW
Whole Collective operates from the belief that well people nurture well relationships, well workspaces, and well communities. We believe in a curious holism approach, a process of courageously getting curious about all parts of ourselves, our relationships, and our impact. Learn more at wholecollective.org.

Smart Gen Society
Founded by Amie Konwinski, Smart Gen Society is a national nonprofit dedicated to empowering smart choices in a digital world. We offer proactive digital education, seminars, resources, and one-on-one services to assist students, caregivers, and community members in protecting their mental health, safety, privacy, and personal brands. Learn more at smartgensociety.org.

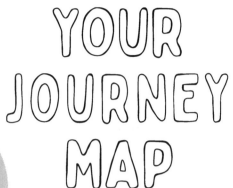

YOUR JOURNEY MAP

Being Social: Understanding the influence, benefits, and power behind social media.

Your Brand: An authentic exploration of what you want from social media and how to create it.

Getting Real: An unedited awareness of your social media use and its influence on your life.

The Tools: Identify and gather the tools you need for a successful pause.

The Plan: Take charge of your personalized plan for healthy boundaries, expectations, and guidelines.

Time to Launch: Seven days of guidance, activities, and reflections to support you through your social media pause.

All the Feels: How to normalize, label, and acknowledge emotions.

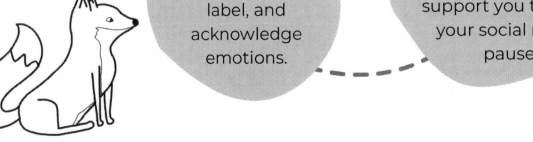

TIMELINE

SUN	MON	TUE	WED	THU	FRI	SAT

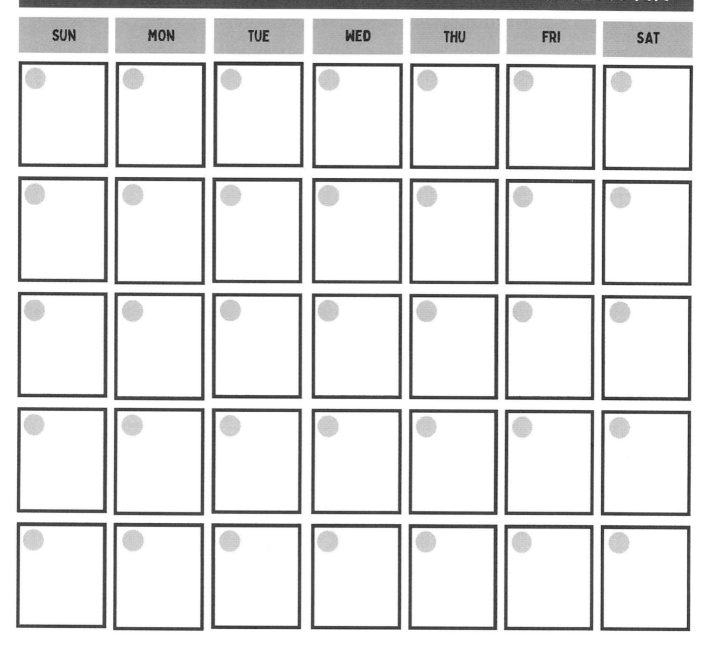

Put it on the calendar! Decide which days you will prepare for your seven days of social media pause. Will you build one skill a day or two? It is up to you! Then decide when your seven-day pause will begin.

BEING
SOCIAL

HEY Y'ALL!

Whether you've found this path on your own, you're participating in a group project, or you've been gifted this book: Welcome!

This journey is filled with activities, coloring, journaling, reflecting, and taking care of yourself. All to support you while you make some changes to the way social media impacts your day-to-day. You might also develop new hobbies, learn a new relaxation strategy, or connect with old friends this week.

The discoveries, connections, and new skills you make will come with all sorts of emotions (and hopefully excitement). However it goes, the week is guided by YOU and for YOU.

WHAT DOES "CONNECTED" FEEL LIKE?

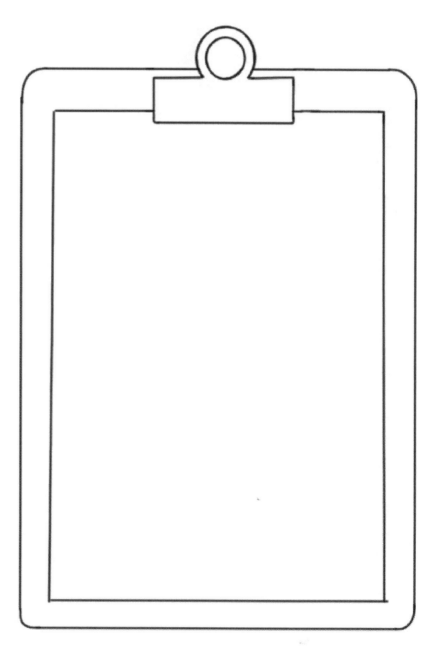

SOCIAL MEDIA HAS UPSIDES AND DOWNSIDES

UPSIDES

Social media offers many benefits.

Social media is a way for us to feel:
- Connected
- Valued
- Entertained
- Seen
- Understood
- A sense of belonging

Social media can be a safe place to exchange thoughts and ideas, find support, and connect with others who share our identities, values, and quirks.

Social media is also entertainment. A place to share our gifts, passions, and thoughts. It's a personal invitation to share our weirdness and uniqueness. An easy way to build a squad, the perfect DIY project, a business, or keep up with a celebrity crush.

DOWNSIDES

For some, social media grows from connection and entertainment into distraction and pressure. What starts as curiosity can quickly develop into comparisons, anxiety, and a habit we cannot stop.

Do you ever feel the need to:
- Consistently check-in
- Create content to feel worthy
- Keep up with streaks
- Entertain others

Does social media impact your:
- Relationships
- Sleep
- School
- Work
- Mental Health

If you say yes to a few of these, it might be time to reevaluate how happy social media is really making you feel.

FEEL GOOD FEELINGS

Have you noticed receiving likes, loves, or comments feels really good? This feel-good feeling is so good! Because we like it, we keep posting, sharing, and selfieing to get more likes, loves, and comments. PHEW! That is a cycle that might be hard to change!

Here's the real deal on feel-so-good feelings...

They are happy hormones and endorphins (a.k.a dopamine, oxytocin, and serotonin*). These endorphins send feel-good messages to our brains, this create feelings of being happy, energized, and connected to life! Pretty cool, right?

Our brains release endorphins and hormones when we do something that brings us joy, excitement, and even fear. We feel alive! It is the rush we feel when we ride a rollercoaster, watch a scary movie, or talk with our crush. That feels good. Without it, we can feel pretty low.

Is your social media use for entertainment or a habit? If it is a habit, it might mean you are seeking to feed the happy chemical you need. If that's what it feels like, no judgement from us! We've all been there. Now that you know, you can use this information to decide if you want to make a change.

_____

Design your feel good feelings.

MY THOUGHTS ON SOCIAL MEDIA

What online supports are important to me?

Skills and hobbies have I explored online...

Online groups or people where I feel included...

Online influencers or entertainment that create laughter...

Is social media the first and last thing I think about every day?

Do I feel like something is missing if I can't check my socials?

Does my mood change based on the number of likes I get?

Does social media affect my sleep?

YOUR
BRAND

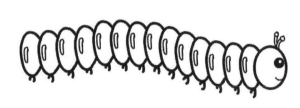

WHAT IS BRAND?

Everyone has a "brand." It is the lasting impression you make. It is how other people get to know you. It is your outward appearance, designed by your habits, choices, and "look." Your brand is developed, cultivated, and shared with the world in your daily interactions and digital spaces - like social media.

Your brand is a unique combination of your:

- Experiences
- Thoughts
- Feelings
- Values
- Favorite activities
- Choices
- Knowledge
- Personality
- Skills
- How you spend your time

The reality is that your brand is constantly evolving. New relationships, experiences, knowledge, and people update your brand. Thinking about your brand might be overwhelming or exciting - or both! No matter the feeling, you always have the power to change your brand or keep it the same.

Design the letters of your name in a font created for you and by you! Elegant and flashy, structured and whimsical... You decide what represents you!

ME AND SOCIAL MEDIA

Ever experience your brand in *digital spaces* looking really different than your brand *in person*?

Sometimes the pressure of who we "should" be on social media pulls us away from who we truly are. When how we choose to spend our time and we post online do not match our values, our brand becomes a little messy and confusing.

Aligning your social media presence, values, and how you spend your time is empowering and affirming. It is a really important part of feeling good about who we are and our relationship with social media.

While you reflect on your brand, let's design something that is ALL about you. Something fabulous! Something grand! Something completely and totally you!

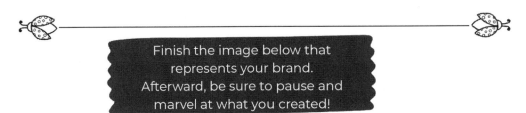

Finish the image below that represents your brand. Afterward, be sure to pause and marvel at what you created!

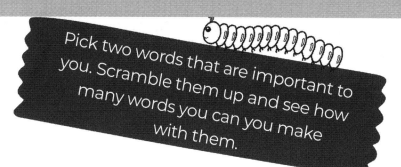

Pick two words that are important to you. Scramble them up and see how many words you can you make with them.

Achievement Beauty Connections Loyalty Relationships
Adventure Creativity Curiosity Friendship Support
Balance Community Kindness Positivity Wisdom

MY VALUES
(Circle all that apply)

Accountability	Connection	Happiness	Learning	Service
Adventure	Contribution	Honesty	Loyalty	Security
Artistic	Courage	Humility	Openness	Sincerity
Assertiveness	Creativity	Humor	Optimism	Spirituality
Athleticism	Curiosity	Independence	Peace	Travel
Authenticity	Determination	Inclusion	Pleasure	Tradition
Balance	Dignity	Influence	Popularity	Status
Beauty	Equality	Inner Harmony	Professionalism	Uniqueness
Belonging	Excellence	Independence	Relationships	Vision
Boldness	Fairness	Justice	Reliablity	Wealth
Challenge	Faith	Leadership	Responsibility	Well-being
Compassion	Gratitude	Fun	Self Respect	Wisdom

MY FAVORITE ACTIVITES
(Circle all that apply)

Acting	Climbing	Film	Robotics	Space
Anime	Coding	Friendships	Running	Spirituality
Animals	Creating	Gaming	Photography	Swimming
Art	Dance	Hiking	Parkour	Traveling
Astronomy	Design	History	Pageants	Videography
Athletics	Digital Arts	Instruments	Politics	Volunteering
Baking	Drama	Languages	Public Speaking	Water Sports
Biking	Drawing	Mathematics	Science	Woodworking
Board Games	Environment	Meditating	Show Choir	Writing
Building	Faith	Movies	Skiing/Boarding	Yoga
Cards	Family	Music	Snorkeling	Other:
Cheer	Fashion	Reading	Social Justice	

MY PEOPLE
List at all of your favorite people and places.

Time to explore your brand and look for the sweet spot!
Make a list of your:
  ° Top five values
  ° Social media sites you spend the most time
  ° As many people, places, and activities as you enjoy!
What do all three areas have in common?

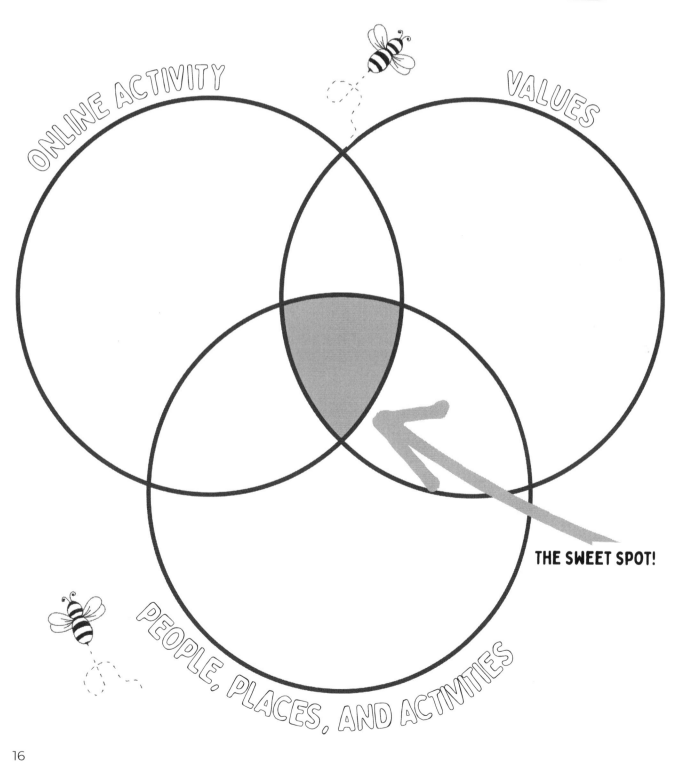

ONLINE ACTIVITY

VALUES

PEOPLE, PLACES, AND ACTIVITIES

THE SWEET SPOT!

ZOOMING IN

So many accounts and not enough time. Getting information about every aspect of others' lives, while sharing our own online can be exhausting. The reality is that this can take a toll on our emotional, mental, and physical health. In the next few pages, let's explore what impact social media has on your life. Let's get reflective, courageous, and REAL.

Write or draw in each star what makes you, YOU! What comes easily and what is challenging for you?

HOW DO I RESPOND TO SOCIAL MEDIA?

1 I notice my phone is a distraction when I am:

Circle the best answer.

with friends	eating	studying	driving
with family	in class	working	relaxing
trying to fall asleep		never	

2 If I receive a text from a friend, I feel I must reply right away.

YES   NO

3 I feel pressure to check my socials hourly.

YES   NO

4 I feel pressure to check my socials daily.

YES   NO

5 For each group of words, choose which phrase you would use to describe how your socials make you feel most of the time.

- Confident
- Kind of confident
- Kind of insecure
- Insecure

- Included
- Kind of included
- Kind of left-out
- Left-out

- Calm
- Kind of calm
- Kind of anxious
- Anxious

- Happy
- Kind of happy
- Kind of sad
- Sad

- Energized
- Kind of energized
- Kind of tired
- Tired

- Intelligent
- Kind of Intelligent
- Kind of unintelligent
- Unintelligent

- Popular
- Kind of popular
- Kind of unpopular
- Unpopular

- Attractive
- Kind of attractive
- Kind of unattractive
- Unattractive

- Safe
- Kind of safe
- Kind of unsafe
- Unsafe

19

6 I use social media or apps to find my friends, see who they are with, or what they are doing.

YES   NO

7 I have been bothered by comments, compliments, pictures, or requests for pictures my socials.

YES   NO

8 Social media has had a POSITIVE impact on the following:

sleep

grades

emotions

physical health

family

friendships

dating

finances

work

none of these

9 Social media has had a NEGATIVE impact on the following:

sleep

grades

emotions

physical health

family

friendships

dating

finances

work

none of these

10 Take a look at the settings on your phone. Open Screentime. What is your Daily Average?

YOU ARE NOT YOUR THOUGHTS

How did it feel to answer questions about the impact of social media? Were you overwhelmed? Enlightened? Surprised? Gathering information about a possible problem is an important part of making a change or taking a pause. It may also be uncomfortable.

At this moment critical self-thoughts might be creeping in. The thoughts running through your mind might not be supportive or kind.

NEWSBREAK!
You are not your thoughts and not all thoughts are facts. Sometimes adjusting or ignoring unsupportive thoughts can change how we feel. Let's try a little self-compassion.

INSTEAD OF...
SELF-CRITICAL

I will fail.

I have to be perfect.

I did something wrong.

WORK TO BE...
SELF-COMPASSIONATE

I can succeed.

I can be myself and make mistakes.

I can learn from this.

WHAT THOUGHTS AM I HAVING RIGHT NOW?
HOW CAN I BE MORE COMPASSIONATE TO MYSELF?

TOOLS YOU'LL NEED

PREP FOR CHANGE

Preparation for change is important and directly impacts success. We want "the plan" of a pause to be successful, an achievement! Let's gather some supplies to make this week fun!

° You will explore new ways of connecting with others
° You will practice new boundaries on your time, space, and emotional energy
° You will explore new feelings
° You will bravely take on the challenge of change

You will be challenged this week. It will be important to surround yourself with people who understand your decision to reduce, change, or pause your relationship with social media and devices.

Use the tape below to list fun you will have this week. What activities bring you joy?

GATHERING SUPPLIES

Fill out each section below.

List supplies you'll need to stay busy.

1 Who am I going to spend time with?

2 What am I going to do?

3 How am I going to stay connected?

- ○ Art or painting supplies
- ○ Make a playlist (or a few!)
- ○ Find a new walking or hiking trail
- ○ Baking or cooking ingredients
- ○
- ○
- ○
- ○
- ○
- ○
- ○
- ○
- ○
- ○
- ○
- ○
- ○
- ○
- ○
- ○
- ○

Here's an idea - Text your besties and let them know you'll be taking a SM pause.

Hey, I am taking a pause from my socials. Can you text me after school instead of snapping?!

TOOLS WORD SEARCH

```
P  K  T  N  C  P  L  S  U  P  W  A  F  N  P  M  Q  C
L  N  F  E  C  A  M  W  L  B  O  O  T  S  M  N  U  T
T  A  Z  L  L  B  M  A  O  E  B  U  R  A  A  J  S  L
R  C  N  I  A  E  W  E  T  O  E  A  V  L  P  P  V  A
M  O  O  T  M  S  S  F  R  C  D  P  C  W  N  G  E  L
R  M  H  K  E  V  H  C  R  A  H  J  I  K  A  D  G  X
C  P  R  R  H  R  G  L  O  X  I  E  R  N  P  T  F  B
Y  A  K  Y  T  E  N  T  I  P  O  B  S  L  G  A  E  R
D  S  L  A  U  P  T  A  R  G  E  M  T  Z  L  B  C  R
P  S  Y  K  G  I  G  Z  E  R  H  Z  X  J  Q  X  A  K
M  A  T  C  A  M  P  F  I  R  E  T  M  K  W  S  B  G
S  N  A  C  K  S  F  C  A  N  T  E  E  N  C  H  Q  G
```

BACKPACK	COMPASS	SLEEPING BAG
BOOTS	FLASHLIGHT	SNACKS
CAMERA	LANTERN	TELESCOPE
CAMPFIRE	MAP	TENT
CANTEEN	MATCHES	WOOD

THE
PLAN

KEEP, REDUCE, OR PAUSE?

This next week will be a discovery of your needs and wants - resetting your relationship with your digital devices and social networks. You will discover new ways to share your energy, ideas, passions, handsome face, and incredible dance moves without your devices. It's possible!

Think about your social media accounts and the reasons you use your digital devices. Also, think about what you have learned in the last few pages. Based on that information, what changes do you want to make?

For example, would you like to keep Snapchat, reduce use, or pause?

○ Keep
○ Reduce
○ Pause

KEEP - MAKE NO CHANGES

REDUCE - TURN OFF NOTIFICATIONS

PAUSE - DELETE FROM DEVICE

On the next page, select your changes, app-by-app.

BUILD YOUR PLAN

You are in charge of your social media pause. If you decide to keep your phone this week - perfect! If you want to turn it off and put it away - perfect! Let's make some decisions about what is right for you. Keep some, reduce all, or pause a little? Use this page to customize your plan. Check all that apply.

- Keep / Reduce / Pause
- text: Keep / Reduce / Pause
- Keep / Reduce / Pause
- Keep / Reduce / Pause
- podcast: Keep / Reduce / Pause
- maps: Keep / Reduce / Pause
- Keep / Reduce / Pause
- Keep / Reduce / Pause
- Keep / Reduce / Pause
- Keep / Reduce / Pause
- Keep / Reduce / Pause
- Keep / Reduce / Pause
- Keep / Reduce / Pause
- What else? Keep / Reduce / Pause
- What else? Keep / Reduce / Pause

29

Design a home screen with your favorite colors, images, or people

11:56   ᵃₒₗᵃₒₗ 📶 50% 🔋

ALL THE
FEELS

FEELING IT

Social media is a big part of our lives. Taking a break could cause insecurity and doubt. When we do something big, we can sometimes have big emotions, and BIG emotions might be new and confusing.

So let's talk about it! Emotions are not "good" or "bad" - although we may have learned to think of them that way. When we label our emotions as positive or negative, we work hard to chase the "good ones" and ignore or avoid the "bad ones." The reality is... emotions are guideposts, like road signs on our path.

When we slow down we can name what we are feeling, are able to ask for support from others, and discover what we need to care for ourselves.

I feel...

because...
(event/activity)

Reflect on what happened that brought on this feeling.

I am also feeling...

Slow down, glance at the feelings list on the next page and explore what else you are experiencing.

I need...

What will calm your mind and/or your body without avoiding what you feel?

Spending our day in different ways might bring a different range of emotions than you're used to. The next few pages list some emotions you might experience during your social media pause.
Check out the feelings list on the next page.

NAME WHAT YOU FEEL

Admiration
Adoration
Affection
Appreciation
Delight
Fondness
Pleasure
Wonder
Regard
Amazed

Amused
Affectionate
Caring
Friendly
Loving
Sympathetic
Warm
Doting
Soft
Tender
Attached
Compassionate

Afraid
Nervous
Dread
Frightened
Cowardly
Terrified
Alarmed
Panicked
Suspicious
Worried
Apprehensive

Agitated
Bothered
Disoriented
Uncomfortable
Uneasy
Irritable
Rash
Offended
Disturbed
Troubled
Grumpy
Unsettled
Unnerved
Restless
Upset

Angry
Furious
Livid
Irritated
Resentful
Hate
Hostile
Aggressive
Worked up
Provoked
Outrage
Defensive

Annoyed
Irritated
Frustrated
Bothered
Impatient
Aggravated
Displeased
Exasperated
Disturbed

Anxious
Distressed
Distraught
Edgy
Fidgety
Frazzled
Irritable
Jittery
Overwhelmed
Restless
Stressed
Preoccupied
Flustered

Confident
Bold
Courageous
Positive
Sure
Fearless
Optimistic
Encouraged
Safe
Powerful
Satisfied
Trusting
Secure
Brave
Empowered

Confused
Lost
disoriented
puzzled
Chaotic
Uncertain
Stuck
Incisive
Foggy
Distraught
Baffled
Flustered
Hesitant
Immobilized
Torn

Disconnected
Lonely
Isolated
Bored
Distant
Removed
Detached
Separate
Broken
Cold
Numb
Rejected
Out of place
Indifferent
Misunderstood
Abandoned

Disgust
Horrified
Dislike
Loathing
Disturbed
Spiteful

Disorganized
Distracted
Bedraggled
Run-Down
Disjointed
Jumbled
Out of sorts

Embarrassment
Awkward
Self-conscious
Silly
Mortified
Humiliated
Flushed
Chagrined
Ashamed
Put down
Guilty
Disgraced

Envy
Jealous
Rivalry
Competitive
Covetous
Resentful
Longing
Insecure
Inadequate
Yearning
Nostalgic
Wistful

Excited
Enthusiastic
Delighted
Amazed
Passionate
Amused
Aroused
Alert
Piqued
Astonished
Dazzled
Energetic
Awakened
Eager
Charged

Exhilarated
Blissful
Ecstatic
Elated
Enthralled
Exuberant
Radiant
Thrilled

Gratitude
Thankful
Grateful
Touched
Moved
Appreciative
Graceful
Responsive
Recognized

Helpless
Paralyzed
Weak
Defenseless
Powerless
Invalid
Abandoned
Alone
Incapable
Useless
Inferior
Vulnerable
Empty
Distressed

Included
Engaged
Understood
Appreciated
Accepted
Acknowledged
Affirmed
Recognized
Welcomed
Connected
Supported
Belonging
Heard
Respected
Involved

Intrigued
Absorbed
Fascinated
Interested
Charmed
Entertained
Captivated
Engrossed
Curious
Surprised

Joyful
Cheerful
Festive
Heartening
Lighthearted
Upbeat
Glad
Merry
Elated
Enjoyable
Euphoria
Slighted
Jubilant
Hopeful
Tickled
Pleased

Pain
Hurt
Remorseful
Disappointed
guilty
Grief
Bereaved
Miserable
Agony
Anguish
Bruised
Crushed
Wounded

Peaceful
Clam
Quiet
Trusting
Fulfilled
Harmonious
Composed
Comfortable
Centered
Content
Relieved
Constant
Mellow
Level
Restful
At Ease

Refreshed
Stimulated
Replenished
Exhilarated
Reinvigorated
Revived
Enlivened
Restored
Liberated
Lively
Passionate
Vibrant
Rested

Sadness
Heartbroken
Hopeless
Regretful
Depressed
Pessimistic
Melancholy
Sorrowful
Morbid
Heavy-hearted
Low
Blue
Gloomy
Miserable
Despair

Stress
Tension
Pressure
Overwhelmed
Frazzled
Strain
Imbalanced
Worried
Uneasy
Cranky
Distraught
Dissatisfied
Weighted Down
Overworked
Pounded
Anxious
Shocked
Frustrated

Tired
Fatigued
Exhausted
Uninterested
Worn out
Fed up
Drained
Weary
Burned out
Lethargic
Beat
Sleepy

Vulnerable
Insecure
Shaky
Open
Unsure
Exposed
Unguarded
Sensitive
Unsafe
Inferior
Raw
Weak
Judged
Inadequate

BOREDOM

"UNSATISFIED WITH AN ACTIVITY" AND "A FEELING OF ENERGY BUT HAVING NOWHERE TO DIRECT THIS ENERGY."

Your courageous decision to take a break from social media has left you with more TIME!! So naturally, you might experience boredom.

  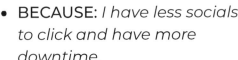  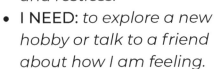   

- **I FEEL:** *bored*
- **BECAUSE:** *I have less socials to click and have more downtime.*
- **I AM ALSO FEELING:** *lonely and restless.*
- **I NEED:** *to explore a new hobby or talk to a friend about how I am feeling.*

I feel...

BORED

because...
(event/activity)

I am also feeling...

I need...

Use the Grid to create a new pattern.

LONELINESS

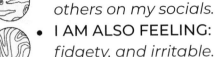
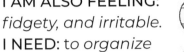

"SADNESS FROM BEING SEPARATE FROM OTHERS: ALONE"

Making a change in the way we connect, like you are doing this week, is courageous and BIG. With your socials, you might be feeling like something is missing or disconnected.

- **I FEEL:** *lonely*
- **BECAUSE:** *I am not connecting with others on my socials.*
- **I AM ALSO FEELING:** *fidgety, and irritable.*
- **I NEED:** *to organize my space and move my body.*

I feel...
LONELY

because...
(event/activity)

I am also feeling...

I need...

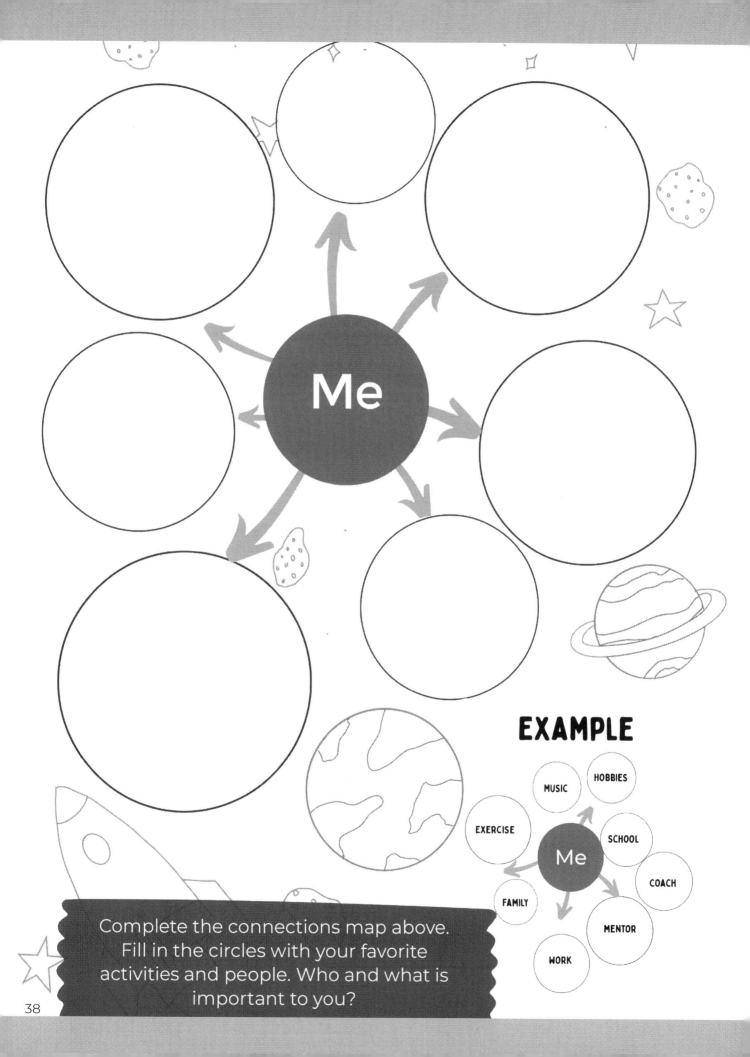

Me

EXAMPLE

MUSIC HOBBIES
EXERCISE SCHOOL
Me
COACH
FAMILY MENTOR
WORK

Complete the connections map above.
Fill in the circles with your favorite
activities and people. Who and what is
important to you?

SADNESS

"FEELINGS OF BEING DOWN, NOT CONTENT, OR SORROW."

Social media gives us instant gratification when we receive likes or supportive comments. Without it, we might feel sad. Remember, there are other ways of feeling this excitement. Let's try to discover what that is this week!

- **I FEEL:** *sad*
- **BECAUSE:** *I don't see likes to my posts or pics.*
- **I AM ALSO FEELING:** *disappointed and unappreciated.*
- **I NEED:** *to do something I am good at, like bake a cake for a friend.*

I feel...

SAD

because...
(event/activity)

I am also feeling...

I need...

Notice three emotions you are feeling right now.
Choose a color to represent each emotion and color
in the images below with each color, filling them to
the intensity of what you are feeling.
If the feelings are BIG, color the container to the brim.

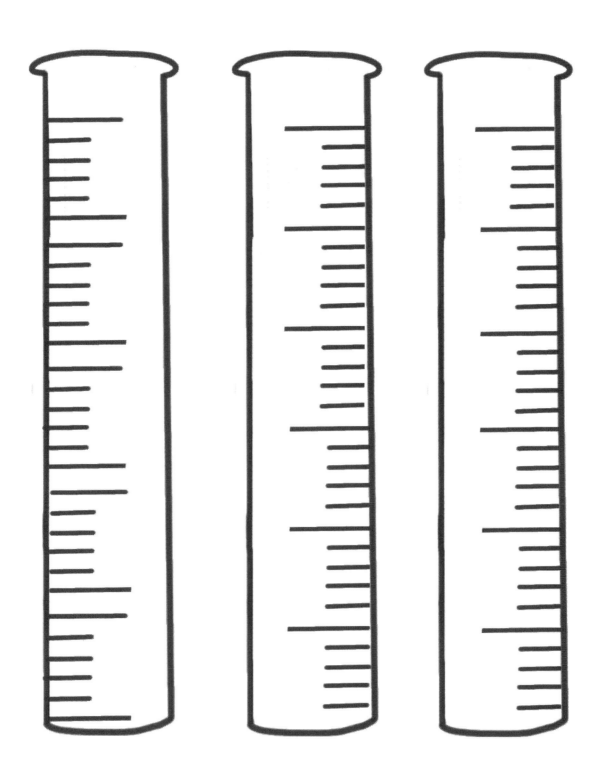

IRRITABLE

"QUICK EXCITABILITY TO ANNOYANCE, IMPATIENCE, OR ANGER."

You are experiencing lots of change this week. Change comes with discomfort - discomfort can cause irritability. Many of us use social media as a way to avoid or distract ourselves from hard feelings.

- **I FEEL:** *irritable*
- **BECAUSE:** *I am less distracted by social media and am noticing new feelings.*
- **I AM ALSO FEELING:** *impatient and uncomfortable.*
- **I NEED:** *to talk with a trusted friend, take a nap and sing at the top of my lungs.*

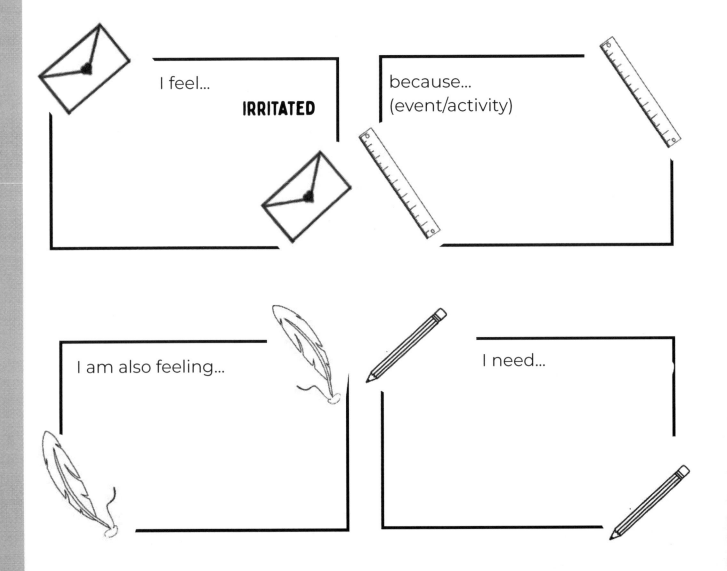

I feel...

IRRITATED

because...
(event/activity)

I am also feeling...

I need...

Find a quiet space, take a few slow breathes. Do you notice any new sounds or smells?

What can you hear?

What can you taste?

What can you touch?

What can you smell?

What can you see?

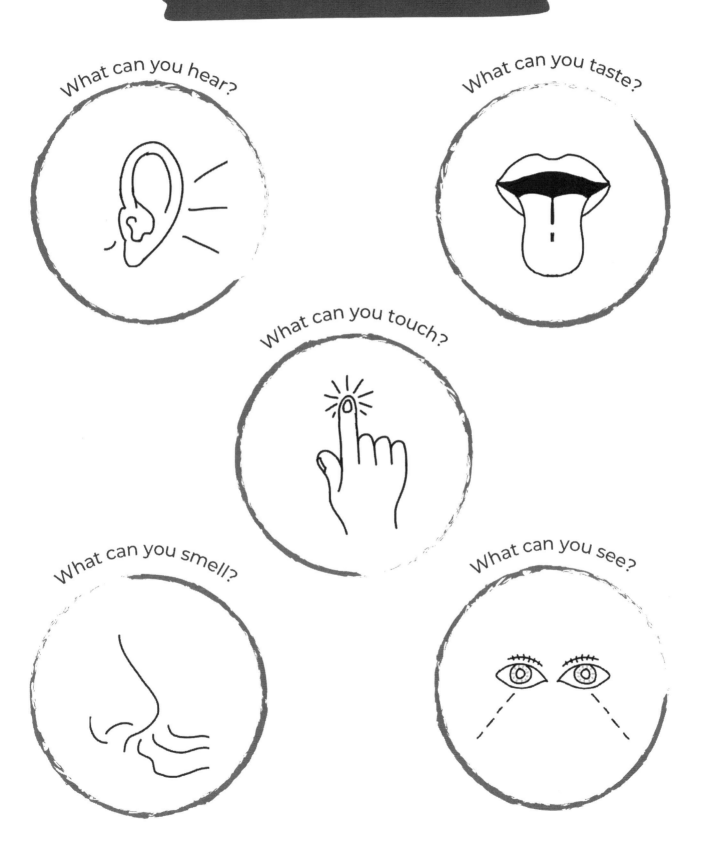

RELIEF

"A FEELING OF REASSURANCE AND RELAXATION FOLLOWING RELEASE FROM ANXIETY OR DISTRESS."

The pressure to respond to all the posts, likes, streaks, and take a perfect selfie - while making sure to share all the important moments in your own life is exhausting! Your break this week takes the pressure off and a sense of relief just might trickle in.

- **I FEEL:** *relief*
- **BECAUSE:** *I don't have pressure to respond.*
- **I AM ALSO FEELING:** *calm and present.*
- **I NEED:** *to listen to my favorite music or podcast or connect with an old friend.*

I feel...

RELIEVED

because...
(event/activity)

I am also feeling...

I need...

Create a reflection! Use color, words, or design that reflects you. Maybe your design is what you see in the mirror or a kind thought you had recently.

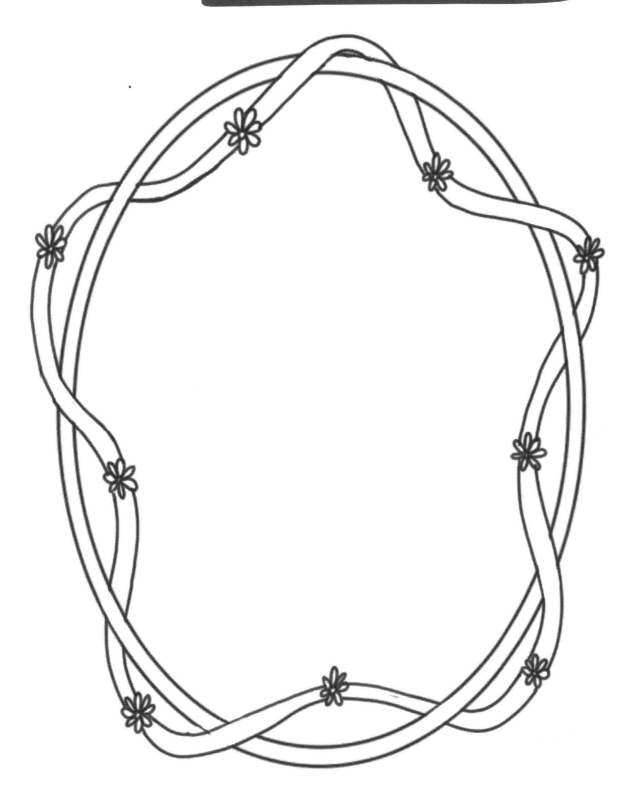

WORRY

"FEAR OF NOT BEING INCLUDED IN SOMETHING OR MISSING OUT."

You have used social media to stay in the know – and without it, you might be experiencing some fear that fun things are happening and you are not included. A little worry of missing out on fun with others or opportunities is normal this week.

- I FEEL: *worried*
- BECAUSE: *I don't see the events or activities of my friends.*
- I AM ALSO FEELING: *overwhelmed and anxious.*
- I NEED: *to take some deep breaths and slow my thoughts.*

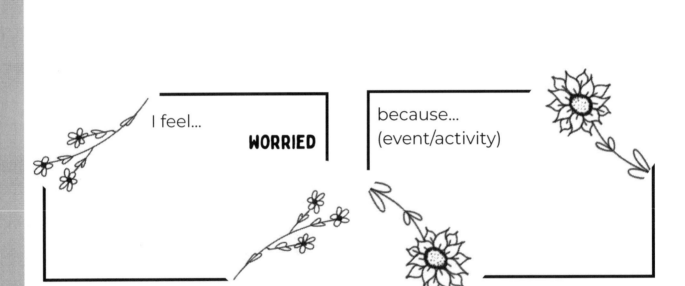

I feel...

WORRIED

because...
(event/activity)

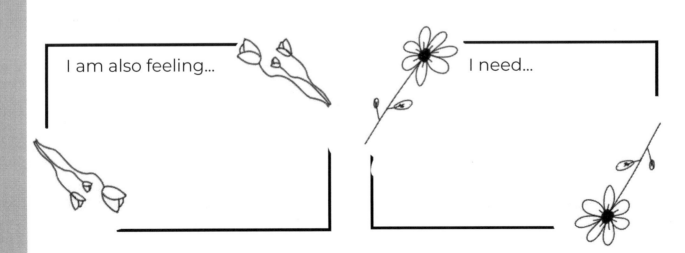

I am also feeling...

I need...

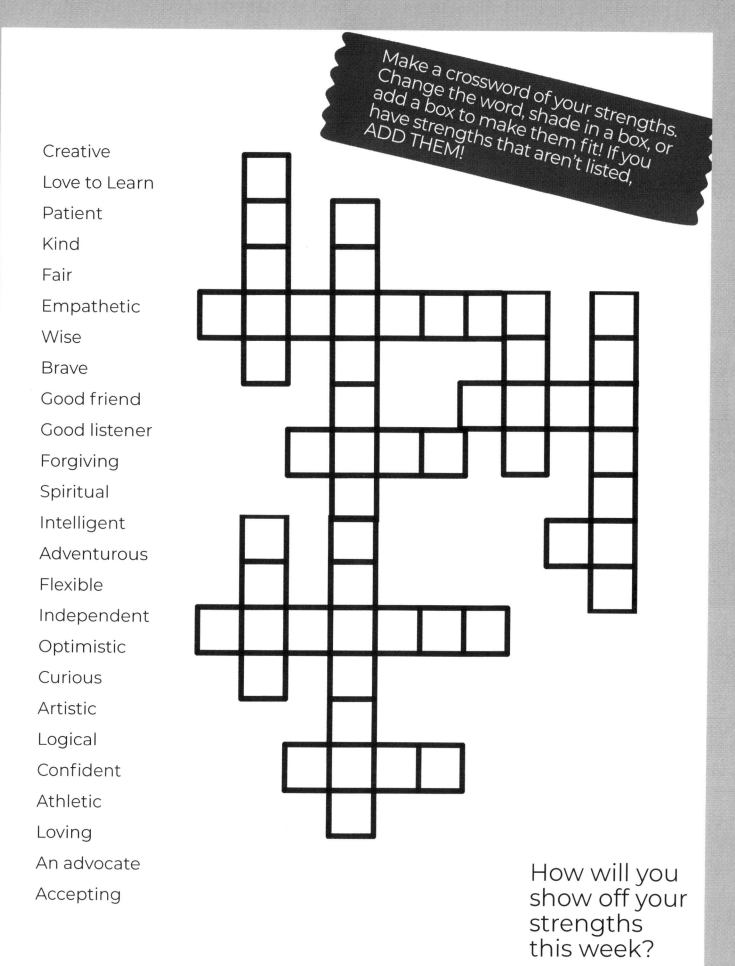

Creative

Love to Learn

Patient

Kind

Fair

Empathetic

Wise

Brave

Good friend

Good listener

Forgiving

Spiritual

Intelligent

Adventurous

Flexible

Independent

Optimistic

Curious

Artistic

Logical

Confident

Athletic

Loving

An advocate

Accepting

Make a crossword of your strengths. Change the word, shade in a box, or add a box to make them fit! If you have strengths that aren't listed, ADD THEM!

How will you show off your strengths this week?

LACK OF FOCUS

"EASILY DISTRACTED" OR "CHALLENGED TO FOCUS ON A SINGULAR TASK."

When we take a break from ANYTHING, we get the sense we are supposed to be doing something more - like we're constantly forgetting something. This can make it hard to be present.

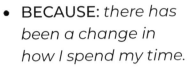

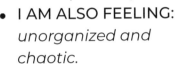

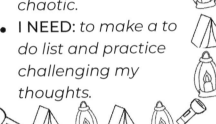

- **I FEEL:** *distracted*
- **BECAUSE:** *there has been a change in how I spend my time.*
- **I AM ALSO FEELING:** *unorganized and chaotic.*
- **I NEED:** *to make a to do list and practice challenging my thoughts.*

I feel...

FOCUSED

because...
(event/activity)

I am also feeling...

I need...

Small pieces come together to create a larger whole. The designs you build in each window pane will come together to create a room with a view. You could be looking into the window or looking out. You decide!

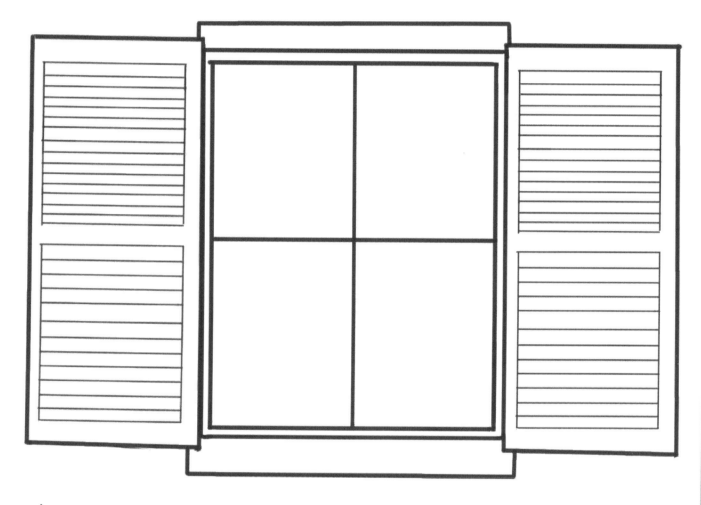

ALL THE FEELS

You can experience more than one emotion at a time.

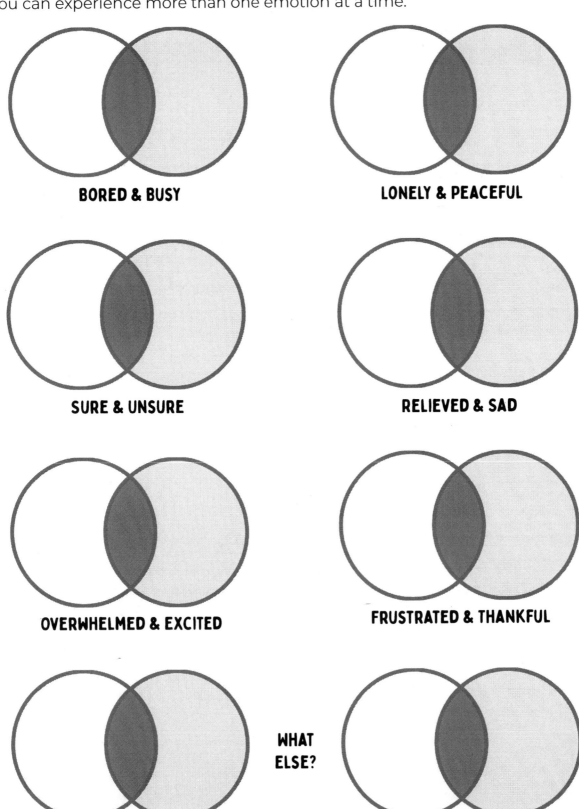

BORED & BUSY

LONELY & PEACEFUL

SURE & UNSURE

RELIEVED & SAD

OVERWHELMED & EXCITED

FRUSTRATED & THANKFUL

WHAT ELSE?

&

&

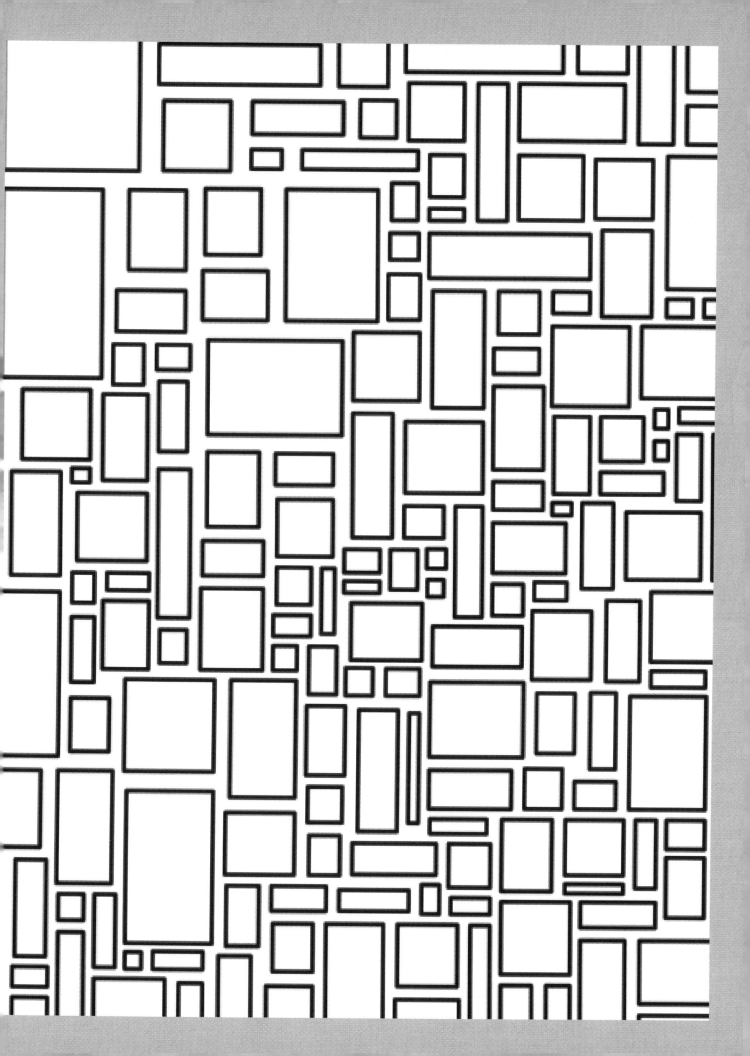

YOU ARE READY

You've done some hard work already. You have reflected on social media's power in your life, you've explored your brand, and where you need some realignment. You've gathered tools, reflected on many emotions, and planned for success this week. KEEP UP THE GOOD WORK!! You are amazing!

At the start of this book, you made a plan. If you need to change the plan you originally designed, that's okay. You now have more information on how to support yourself during your pause week. Use the timeline below to build a plan with support and activities. Maybe on day four you plan a day with friends or read a good book. Let's write it down!

Whatever your plan, there are three things main areas of focus:
° Accept feelings without judgment
° Try something new or reconnect with an old hobby
° Stay connected or reconnect with your people

TIMELINE   PAUSE CALENDAR

SUN	MON	TUE	WED	THU	FRI	SAT

LET'S DO THIS

For the next seven days, use the guidance, activities, and reflections to support you through your social media pause. You've practiced and prepared for this. You are ready!

Remember that your pause and self-care this week is an act of self-love. You are human and worthy. We hope you understand slowing down to care for yourself is essential.

Your thoughts, emotions, and body all play an important role in taking care of yourself. Every day you will spend time with your thoughts, feelings and check in with your body. Developing the ability to take care of your mind, heart, and body during times of change and stress is a way to commit to everyday wellness. Take what you have loved about these next seven days and do them again and again. Leave the rest behind!

THE NEXT SEVEN DAYS

For the next seven days, your activity journey will be about creating, reflecting, journaling, and noticing your body. Each day will offer three activities: a journal prompt, a personal reflection to do alone or with friends, and a guided mindfulness activity. Keep an eye out for the special reminders to connect others and in nature.

1 DAILY JOURNAL PROMPT
Write it out! Draw it Out! No need for perfection or complete sentences (unless you love complete sentences). No judgment or corrections needed.

2 DAILY REFLECTION
Daily Reflection Question- Pause and make some time to spend with YOU. Find a quiet space...OR... gather with friends and reflect together.

3 DAILY MINDFULNESS ACTIVITY
Practice noticing how your body feels this week. We've included a QR code that directs you to a recorded script for guidance each day.

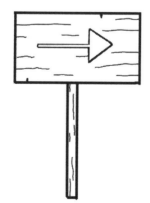

**EXPLORE OUTSIDE AND
CONNECT WITH NATURE!**

WHAT WILL YOU FIND?

DAY 1

JOURNAL PROMPT

FIND SOMETHING SMOOTH & SOFT

What I am giving up this week? Write a goodbye letter.

Create a color wheel. Select feelings from the feelings list and label the color that represents what that emotion feels like to you.

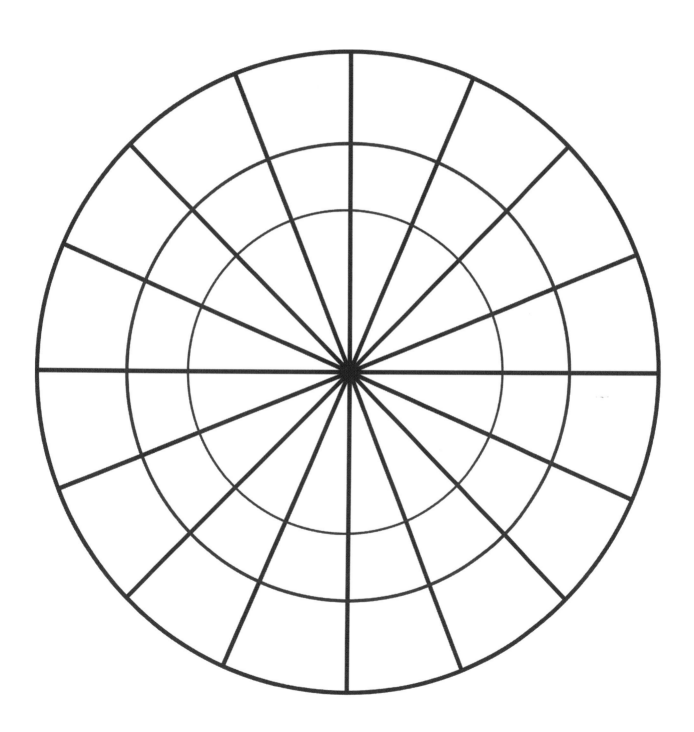

BELLY BREATH

A practice to ground ourselves in this moment. When we are overwhelmed it can be challenging to be present. Long, slower breathes can reduce anxiety, slow rapid thoughts, and increase oxygen to our bloodstream.

TODAY'S REFLECTION QUESTION.

Today, I give myself permission to feel..."

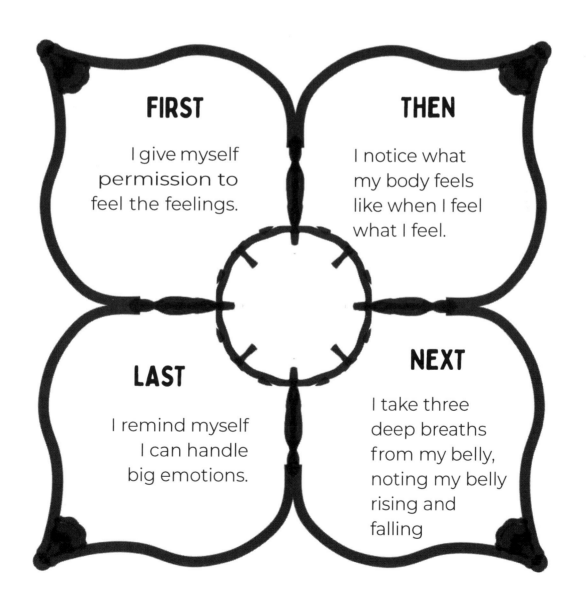

FIRST

I give myself permission to feel the feelings.

THEN

I notice what my body feels like when I feel what I feel.

LAST

I remind myself I can handle big emotions.

NEXT

I take three deep breaths from my belly, noting my belly rising and falling

DAY 2

JOURNAL PROMPT

What is one hobby or skill I want to rediscover this week? Why is this important? How will I do it?

TODAY'S REFLECTION QUESTION.

"When I experience big or overwhelming emotions, I tend to. . ."

Using the design below, create something BIG and REGAL!

PAUSE AND MAKE SOME TIME TO SPEND WITH YOU. FIND A QUIET SPACE...OR... GATHER WITH FRIENDS AND REFLECT TOGETHER.

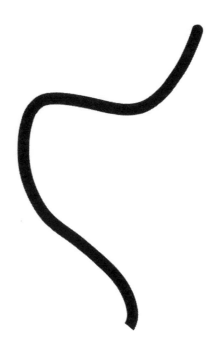

RELAX YOUR ENTIRE BODY

A practice to release tension in your body, which can work to calm our minds. With a calm mind, we can learn to let go of the things we no longer need creates more space for ourselves to fully feel who and where we are.

> Think about all the parts that make creatures unique, wings to fly or long legs to run fast. Create some bugs with super parts, parts that make them unique and built to survive difficult conditions.

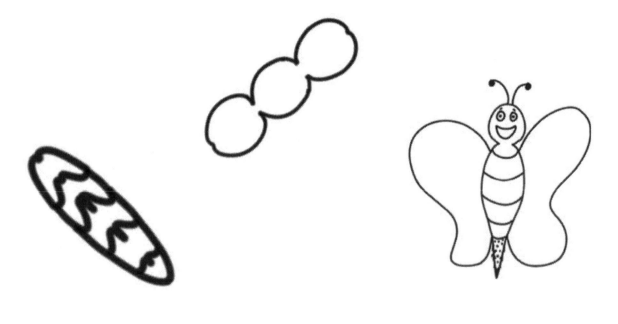

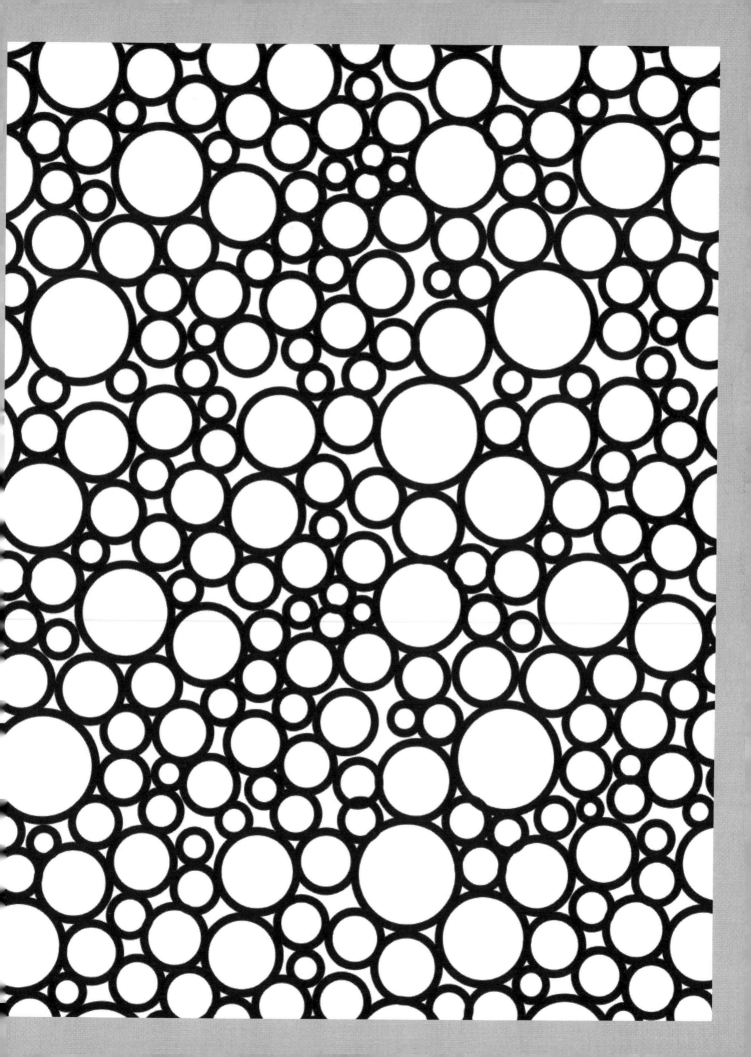

DAY 3

JOURNAL PROMPT

FIND SOMETHING WITH SPARKLE

When am I the most ME? Who am I with? What am I doing?

TODAY'S REFLECTION QUESTION.

The last time I remember saying "yes" when I wanted to say "no", I felt..."

Create or design a space that is safe, warm, and you feel free to be you. It could be a treehouse, a boathouse, or a cozy cave. You decide!

PAUSE AND MAKE SOME TIME TO SPEND WITH YOU. FIND A QUIET SPACE...OR... GATHER WITH FRIENDS AND REFLECT TOGETHER.

BODY BOUNDARIES MEDITATION

A practice to envision the boundaries of your own personal space. It empowers you to hold space for yourself.

> How many boxes can you create? Same size or different sizes, make as many boxes as you can.

Setting personal boundaries is all about you. Say "no" when you need time and space, and "yes" when you want connection or opportunity.

DAY 4

JOURNAL PROMPT

FIND SOMETHING GREEN OR GOLD

What have I needed this week to feel connected, loved, or valued?
Was it easy to ask for what I needed? Why or Why not?

TODAY'S REFLECTION QUESTION.

Imagine you have a magic wand and when you wave it you no longer need to listen to what people say you "should" do or how you "should" act. How have you changed? How have you stayed the same?

PAUSE AND MAKE SOME TIME TO SPEND WITH YOU. FIND A QUIET SPACE...OR... GATHER WITH FRIENDS AND REFLECT TOGETHER.

Turn on your favorite song, put your pen on the page and let the music guide your drawing. Do not lift your pen from the page until the music stops. Admire what you have created!

SEED MEDITATION

This is an exercise to help you consider what you and how you need to nurture yourself.

Create a super plant! Give your plant a name. What does it need to thrive?
Does your plant have powers or a nemesis?

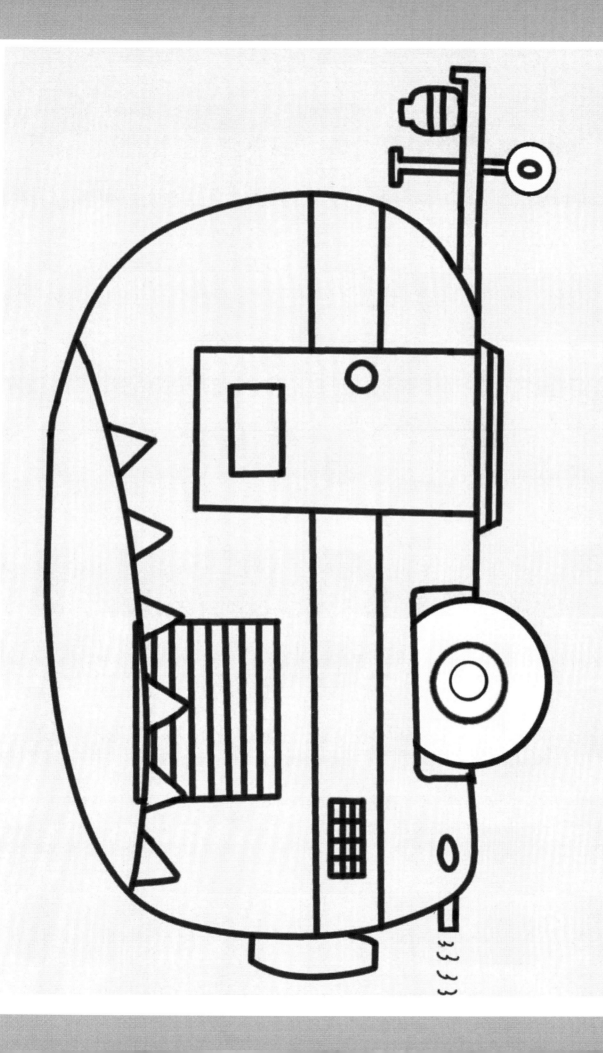

DAY 5

JOURNAL PROMPT

FIND A SINGING BIRD

Make a list of what brings joy or comfort to your senses. What do you hear, taste, smell, touch, and see?

TODAY'S REFLECTION QUESTION.

What time of day has been most difficult during your pause? Is it during your wake up or your slow down, or somewhere in between?

PAUSE AND MAKE SOME TIME TO SPEND WITH YOU. FIND A QUIET SPACE...OR... GATHER WITH FRIENDS AND REFLECT TOGETHER.

All feelings are valid. Create an anger or stress design. Choose colors that represent your stress, anger, frustration or irritability. Scribble, write, and get messy.

TREE POSE

This is a guided practice that focuses on rooting into the ground to find balance and stability.

Complete the trees with your words, colors, and images. Whatever you choose is perfect!

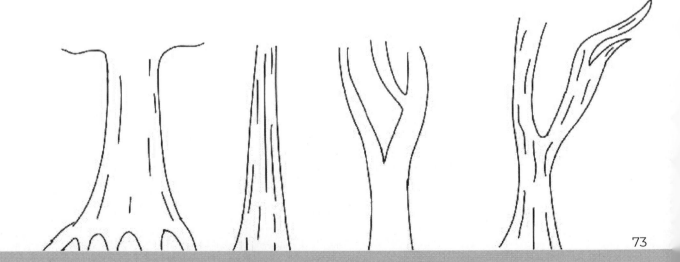

DAY 6

JOURNAL PROMPT

FIND ANIMALS IN THE CLOUDS

What changes have I made to how I spend my time? Has it changed how I have interacted with myself, my family, and my friends or my peers?

TODAY'S REFLECTION QUESTION.

What did I expect to experience this week?
What surprised me or was unexpected?

PAUSE AND MAKE SOME TIME TO SPEND WITH YOU. FIND A QUIET SPACE...OR... GATHER WITH FRIENDS AND REFLECT TOGETHER.

THE EXPECTED

THE UNEXPECTED

STICKY SPOTS MEDITATION

This body scan helps you notice and "breathe in" to places in your body that are holding stress, pain, or resentment.

Use different colors to represent how you body feels. Do you have spots that hold tension or a place for calm?

DAY 7

JOURNAL PROMPT

FIND A SPOT OUTSIDE TO LAY DOWN

Write a letter to yourself from yourself, like you are your own best friend.
What do you need to hear to feel encouraged, safe and loved?

TODAY'S REFLECTION QUESTION.

Revisit the feelings list on page 34-35. What emotions are you experiencing today? Get curious and accepting of the emotions you feel today. Share it with a friend.

PAUSE AND MAKE SOME TIME TO SPEND WITH YOU. FIND A QUIET SPACE...OR... GATHER WITH FRIENDS AND REFLECT TOGETHER.

Describe through words, images and color what it feels like to be you today.

HEART STRING MEDITATION

This is a guided practice of finding what energy you're holding that is yours vs. someone else's. It walks you through finding ways to let go of what you no longer wish to carry.

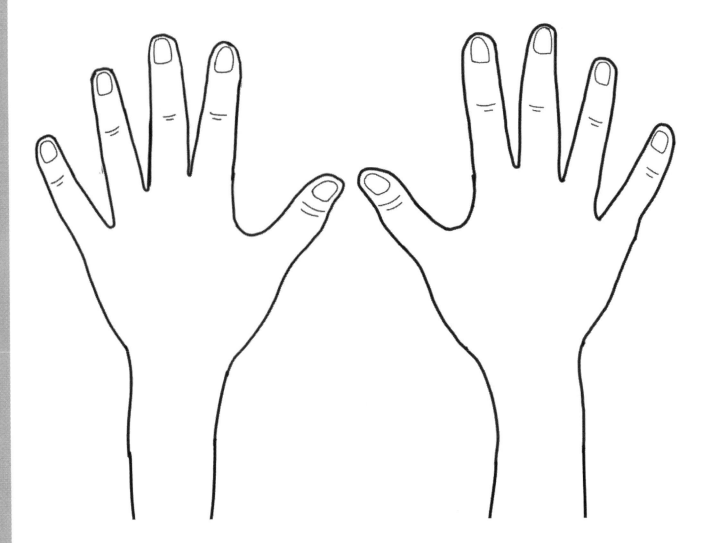

Using color and words, explore what you want to hold on to and let go of from your experience this week.

SUCCESS THIS WEEK

YOUR THOUGHTS, EMOTIONS, AND BODY ALL PLAY AN IMPORTANT ROLE IN TAKING CARE OF YOURSELF. IN THE LAST SEVEN DAYS, YOU CONNECTED WITH PEOPLE AND ACTIVITIES AND PRIORITIZED YOUR NEEDS. MAP OUT YOUR SUCCESSES THIS WEEK!

Here some questions to get you started...

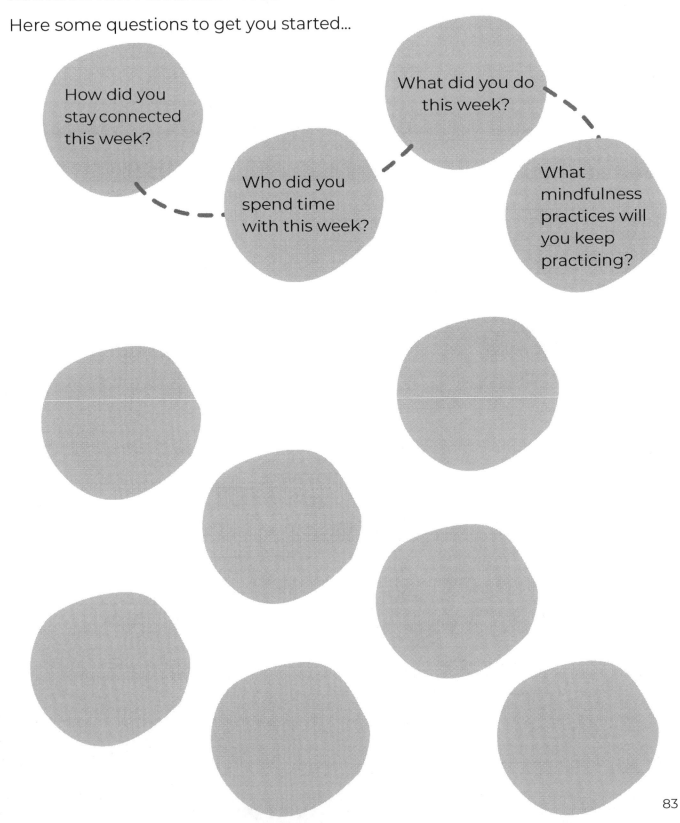

How did you stay connected this week?

Who did you spend time with this week?

What did you do this week?

What mindfulness practices will you keep practicing?

83

IN THE LAST 7 DAYS...

DAY 1	DAY 2	DAY 3	DAY 4	DAY 5	DAY 6	DAY 7

Give each day of your pause a review by coloring in the stars. 5 stars is a great day! Make a note of what part of the day was the most difficult and when the week began to feel less difficult.

84

You have a new understanding of the influence, benefits, and power of social media in your life.

LOOK WHAT YOU ACCOMPLISHED!

You got honest and courageous and have an unedited awareness of your social media use and its influence.

You have begun to build and adjust an authentic brand online and in life.

You created and took charge of personalized plan for to set healthy boundaries with social media.

You identified and gathered tools to support you while doing something new and difficult.

You explored, and validated uncomfortable feelings and identified new ways to care for self.

You reflected, journaled, and checked in with your body, even when it was hard.

HEY Y'ALL!

You completed the preparation, practice and pause! Whether you've worked on this alone or with a group--you have done some really great work. Maybe the activities, reflecting, and taking care of yourself this week was new to you or maybe they were something you were already pretty good at. Regardless-- YOU DID IT!

The next steps in your relationship with social media are yours to make. You can take any of the activities, reflections, new hobbies, relaxation strategies, and insight into how to care for yourself during difficult emotions with you. They are yours to keep. You earned them. Use them whenever you need to feel more connected to yourself or others, need a realignment with your values, explore and tend to emotions. The skills you built this week can be used whenever you need to do the next hard thing.

Keep taking great care of yourself.

Jessyca, Alicia, Katie

PREPARATION, PRACTICE AND PAUSE...

 COMPLETE.

THE CREATORS

JESSYCA (SHE/HER)

A social worker, a clinician and social justice advocate. She loves lifting weights, creative writing, and traveling with her daughters. Jessyca is the mother of five humans, three dogs, a cat, and six chickens.

ALICIA (SHE/HER)

A mother, dancer, social worker, therapist, and trained yoga instructor living in Omaha, NE. She loves hiking, traveling, art history, and anything on Disney+ with Marvel or Star Wars.

AMIE (SHE/HER)

A mama to five girlies, Navy veteran (CPO), media use expert, national keynote speaker, and CEO. In her free time, she enjoys adventure travel, hiking, water sports, and board games.

THE ILLUSTRATOR

KATIE (SHE/HER)

A senior in high school with plans to study at a four year institution. She loves softball, math, crocheting, baking (including the process of laminating croissant dough (IYKYK), her dog Stache, CrossFit and any episode of Criminal Minds!

REFERENCES AND RESOURCES

MORE ABOUT SEROTONIN, DOPAMINE SOCIAL MEDIA ADDICTION"
Harvard Medical School
health.harvard.edu/mind-and-mood/serotonin-the-natural-mood-booster
Stanford Medicine
scopeblog.stanford.edu/2021/10/29/addictive-potential-of-social-media-explained

ADAPTED FEELINGS LIST""
Mental Health America
mhanational.org

MORE ABOUT HOW THE ACTIVITY JOURNEY FOR SOCIAL MEDIA PAUSE WAS DEVELOPED
ketv.com/article/ketv-challenge-teens-discover-better-sleep-less-anxiety-and-more-fun-after-week-off-social-media/38324775#

MENTAL HEALTH SUPPORT
National Suicide Prevention Line: Call or Text 988
LifeLine Chat: suicidepreventionlifeline.org/chat
Trevor Project offers call, text, and chat support: thetrevorproject.org

Made in the USA
Columbia, SC
13 January 2023

10203489R00050